ADRENALINE RUSH

BMX BIKING

AJ ANDERSON

A⁺

Smart Apple Media

Published by Smart Apple Media,
an imprint of Black Rabbit Books
P.O. Box 3263, Mankato, Minnesota 56002
www.blackrabbitbooks.com

Printed in Printed in the United States
of America at Corporate Graphics,
North Mankato, Minnesota.

Published by arrangement with the Watts
Publishing Group LTD, London.

Library of Congress Cataloging-in-Publication Data

Anderson, A. J.
BMX biking / AJ Anderson.
p. cm.—(Adrenaline rush)
Includes index.
Summary: "Explains the basics of BMX
biking, including the different styles, the
equipment needed, and history of the sport.
Also features biographies on several famous
BMX riders"—Provided by publisher.
ISBN 978-1-59920-681-3 (library binding)
1. Bicycle motocross—Juvenile literature. I. Title.
GV1049.3.A64 2013
796.62—dc23
                                2011032613

PO1433
2-2012

9 8 7 6 5 4 3 2 1

Picture credits:
t–top, b–bottom, l–left, r–right, c–center
front cover Homydesign/Dreamstime.com, back
cover Melhi/Istockphoto.com, 1 Peter Kim/
Dreamstime.com, 4br Mishella/Shutterstock, 5
Kristina Postnikova/Shutterstock.com, 6–7
Homydesign/Dreamstime.com, 7tr Getty Images,
8b Qik/Shutterstock, 9 Fei Maohua/Xinhua Press/
Corbis, 9bl Wikicommons, 10b Sheldon Ivester/
istockphoto.com, 11 Michel Stevelmans/
Shutterstock.com, 12 Tomasz Trojanowski/
Shutterstock.com, 13tr Igor Jandric/Dreamstime.
com, 13br Warren Price/Dreamstime.com, 14
Mishella/Shutterstock.com, 15tl Mike Thomas/
Dreamstime.com, 15bl Wikicommons, 16 Peter
Kim/Dreamstime.com, 17t Zepherwind/
Dreamstime.com, 18 Cruskoko/Dreamstime.com,
19cr wrangler/Shutterstock.com, 19bl courtesy of
Red Bull, 20–21 Photoroller/Dreamstime.com, 21cl
Suzanne Tucker /Shutterstock.com, 21bl Peter
Kim/Dreamstime.com, 22b Timothy Large/
Shutterstock.com, 23 Timothy Large/Shutterstock.
com, 23bl GNU, 24br Timothy Large/Shutterstock.
com, 25 Timothy Large/Shutterstock.com, 25tr
Bloomberg/Getty Images, 26–27 Sergey
Lavrentev/Dreamstime.com, 27t Martin Lehmann/
Shutterstock.com, 27br Olga Popova/Dreamstime.
com, 28–29 Rkaphotography/Dreamstime.com,
27tr Cszmurlo/GNU

Disclaimer
The website addresses (URLs) included in this
book were valid at the time of going to press.
However, because of the nature of the Internet, it
is possible that some addresses have changed, or
sites may have changed or closed down since
publication. While the author and publisher regret
any inconvenience this may cause to readers, no
responsibility for any such changes can be
accepted either by the author or the publisher.

In preparation of this book, all due care has been
exercised with regard to the advice, activities, and
techniques depicted. The publishers regret that
they can accept no liability for any loss or injury
sustained. When learning a new activity, it is
important to get expert advice and to follow a
manufacturer's instructions.

Words in **bold** are in the glossary on page 30.

CONTENTS

BMX is simple. It is just you and the most basic bike you can imagine: a small, strong frame with just one gear, two little wheels, and not much more. There are no distractions—you can concentrate on the fun of riding.

Expert BMXers have a massive range of tricks. Sometimes, like this rider, they barely stay in contact with the bike while in the air.

The Joy of BMX

Anyone who has ridden a BMX bike knows that they are very satisfying to ride. The bikes are so small that they are really easy to move around. Jumps, spins, hops, and other tricks are much easier to do on a BMX than on a big bike.

The thrills of BMX are addictive. It will not take long after your first time on a BMX before you are rolling down to a skatepark and eyeing up the ramp.

Do not try this unless a) you are a really good biker or b) you want to swim and your bike needs a wash!

Top Three BMX Movies
- BMX Bandits—the cheesy 1980s plotline cannot disguise a great movie. Watch out for an appearance by a very, very young Nicole Kidman.
- Miracle Boy and Nyquist—a documentary starring legends Dave "Miracle Boy" Mirra and Ryan Nyquist.
- BMX Crash!—a collection of some of the most spectacular (and painful) BMX crashes ever filmed.

Sharing the Thrill

BMXing is popular around the world. If you are into BMXing, wherever there is concrete you will have somewhere to ride. You will also find people to ride and share tricks with. A friendly smile and a hello will get you a warm welcome at most places where BMXers hang out.

BMX is short for Bicycle Motocross. It became popular in the 1970s, when riders would race road bikes around motocross tracks. These riders may have been inspired by the motorcycle racing film *On Any Sunday* (see page 7), but they did not have motorcycles to race.

The Spread of BMX

By the mid-1970s, the word had got out, and bikers everywhere were realizing how much fun it was to race a bike around a bumpy, jump-filled dirt track. Empty lots and spare fields suddenly found a new use as BMX **circuits**. The first BMX world championships were held in 1982.

Today's BMX bikes have much stronger frames than the old Stingray bikes, whose frames would probably break if you performed this kind of trick on them.

Death of the Stingray

Most early BMXers rode a bike called a Stingray. The bikes were customized to look like off-road motorcycles. Stingrays were not really built for off-road use and they would often snap in half while riders were racing them! Soon, tougher bikes similar to today's BMX bikes began to appear.

These two riders from the 1960s are right to be looking proud of their Stingray bikes, complete with banana seats and big, chrome handlebars.

BMX Bombs

By the end of the 1980s, the BMX craze had died out. The sport had become very competitive, with most attention focused on racing leagues. If you did not want to race, BMX did not have much to offer you. Just a few enthusiasts were keeping the BMX flame burning.

On Any Sunday
The documentary On Any Sunday was released in 1971. It was made by the filmmaker Bruce Brown, who was already famous for his surfing movie, The Endless Summer. On Any Sunday was a massive hit, partly because one of the racers featured was the motorcycle fanatic and movie star Steve McQueen. It explored the world of dirt bike racing, and is said to have been one of the big reasons why BMX became popular.

In the 1990s, BMX started to make a comeback. But this time the sport was different. Riders were not really interested in racing around dirt tracks. Instead, they were hungrily eyeing up the new skateparks that had started to appear, prompted by the rebirth of skateboarding around the same time.

Racers pour down one of the biggest start ramps in BMX racing at the 2008 Beijing Olympics (right).

Freestyle BMX

Today, the most popular form of BMX, freestyle, has nothing to do with racing. Instead it relies on bike-control skills to perform tricks, and it is divided into:

- street—doing tricks on obstacles that are not really designed for riding. These include stairs and handrails.

- vert and park—which take place on specially built ramps, usually in a skatepark.

- dirt jumping—leaping over specially built dirt ramps.

- flatland—doing all kinds of tricks on a smooth, flat surface, such as standing on the foot pegs while spinning the handlebars around.

Role Models

The new wave of BMXers looked up to riders, such as Mat Hoffman, who were inventing new skatepark tricks. Hoffman alone has invented more than 100 BMX tricks. He has also helped many of the sport's other top riders to develop, including Dave Mirra, Jay Miron, and Kevin Jones.

There is still a BMX race scene, and the sport is now featured at the Olympic Games. Many of the top racers, however, come from track cycling or mountain biking backgrounds.

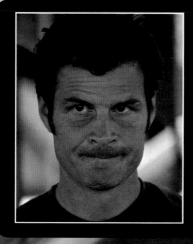

Mat Hoffman is called "The Condor" because of his ability to soar high into the air like a bird on his BMX. He is probably the best vert rider in the history of the sport. Hoffman was a star from his first professional appearance at the age of 15, in 1987. He was still pushing the boundaries at the 2002 X Games, where he completed the first-ever competition **no-hands 900**.

MAT HOFFMAN

BMXers have to put a lot of trust in their bikes. As they jump, spin, or hop, they need to know that the bike will not give out underneath them. That is why BMXers almost always buy the best bike they can afford.

The Ideal Bike

The key requirement for a BMX bike is that it should be strong. After all, you are going to be putting it under a lot of stress and strain, and you do not want it to break! The ideal bike should also be light enough to throw around during tricks and while ramp riding.

Handlebars (1), cranks (2), chains (3), and cogs (4) are all designed with toughness in mind.

Frames are smaller than other kinds of bike. This makes it easier to do tricks.

Wheel rims and tires are thick and strong to prevent buckled wheels and punctures.

Most frames are made of steel, which is strong. Even if it is dented, it can be repaired. Some race frames are made of aluminum or carbon fiber, which are lighter than steel.

Most BMXers ride their bikes as **single speeds** using a **freewheel**. A few riders, though, ride **fixed**, especially when performing flatland tricks.

This trick, known as "walking the dog" shows why BMX bikes need to be light but strong!

Small wheels have plenty of spokes for strength. Most BMXs have 20 in. (508 mm) wheels, though some have 24 in. (610 mm) wheels, which are just 2 in. (51 mm) smaller than those on a mountain bike.

Pegs are used during tricks and grinds (sliding the bike along a surface, such as a ledge).

Used Machines
Buying a secondhand BMX is risky because the bike might have been crashed or damaged. Some of the parts might be worn out. Always:
• take a skilled mechanic with you to look at a used bike, to see if anything needs to be replaced.
• ask the seller to show you a receipt showing when the bike was bought. This will make sure it was not stolen.

Apart from the bike, little equipment is needed for BMX biking. The most important piece of equipment is a helmet—many skateparks do not let people ride unless they are wearing one. Pads and gloves can also be useful for certain kinds of riding.

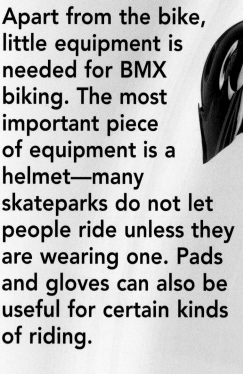

Helmet
*Most riders wear a simple open face helmet. A few use **full-face helmets** like this one, which also protects the chin. All helmets need to be fastened snugly so that they will not come off in a crash.*

Elbow and knee pads
In any kind of crash, your elbows and knees are vulnerable. Pads are particularly important for ramp riding, when the riders sometimes jump high into the air—the world record is more than 50 feet (15 m)!

This rider is wearing flat soled shoes, which will help his feet grip the pedals.

Gloves
These are usually reinforced to offer extra protection to the knuckles and palms of the rider's hands.

Clothing and Other Equipment

The clothes people wear for BMX need to be tough and comfortable. It is a mistake to ride in your best jeans because they are bound to get ripped. Few riders wear lots of layers—the riding gets them hot quickly enough! Flat shoes are best. They grip the pedals well, but can be moved easily without catching your heel.

Lots of riders carry a backpack with them. It is a useful place to store things while you are riding, such as a cell phone, clothes you have taken off, money, water, and simple bike tools.

Clothing should be loose to keep you cool on a hot day. It shouldn't be too loose, however, or there is a danger that it will get caught in the bike.

Extra Protection
Some riders wear extra protection, especially if they are going for a new, dangerous trick or are racing:
- *neck braces (pictured left)—fit around the neck to support the head and help to stop serious neck injuries.*
- *body armor—sheets of tough plastic to protect the ribs and kidneys.*
- *mouth guards—stop teeth being damaged in a crash.*

HELPFUL HINTS

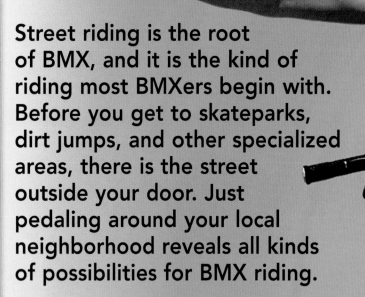

Street riding is the root of BMX, and it is the kind of riding most BMXers begin with. Before you get to skateparks, dirt jumps, and other specialized areas, there is the street outside your door. Just pedaling around your local neighborhood reveals all kinds of possibilities for BMX riding.

Opportunities, not Obstacles

If you are walking, low walls, curbs, benches, and stairs can be a bit of an obstacle, slowing down your journey. On a BMX, however, these are opportunities for tricks:

• A low concrete wall might offer the chance to do a **grind**, sliding the pegs along the top.

• A curb is a good place to do an **endo**, stopping the front wheel against the curb and letting the back wheel rise up.

• A bench might be a good challenge for practicing your jumping skills.

• Stairs offer more opportunities for grinds or jumps.

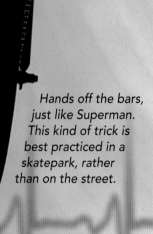

Hands off the bars, just like Superman. This kind of trick is best practiced in a skatepark, rather than on the street.

Street Riding in the, um… Park

Most skateparks have street areas where BMXers can practice their street skills. These can be great places to learn new tricks. There will probably be other riders there who can give you some tips, and there is zero chance of security guards or grumpy people telling you to clear out.

This rider makes a good clearance in a skatepark high jump contest.

Top Two Street Movies
- Can I Eat—*the best street tricks by some of the world's greatest street riders, including Vinnie Sammon, Tyrone Williams, Steven Hamilton, and plenty of others.*
- Refresh—*filmed over 18 months, this film documents the riders from the BMX street scene in Seattle, and the spots they ride.*

ON THE SCREEN

Reynolds won his first top-level BMX contest at the age of 12, when he took first place in the Taz Tour. He turned professional a year later, and within a few years was one of the world's top street and ramp riders. There are rumors that in May 2010, he successfully landed a **900 bar spin** on a **quarter pipe**.

GARRETT REYNOLDS

Ramp riding is probably the most spectacular form of BMX. Skilled riders include bar spins, **no-hands** tricks, and even loops in their rides. For ordinary mortals, it is usually enough just to avoid crashing.

After landing a big aerial trick, this BMXer pushes his bike back into line off the back wheel before riding down the ramp.

Ramp Rules

The three rules for ramp riding are:

• always wait your turn.

• never cut across another rider.

• stand back from the top of the ramp while someone else is riding.

Moves like this cross-up add difficulty to tricks, and earn you a higher competition score.

Types of Ramps

There are three main kinds of ramps:

- mini ramps—riders learn basic ramp-riding skills on mini ramps, which are usually lower than 6.5 feet (2 m). Crashing on a mini ramp may be painful, but probably will not be life-threatening.

- **vert ramps**—these are usually bigger than mini ramps, and have vertical walls. Vert ramps allow the riders to launch massive **air** after massive air. Riders soar so high that they have time to finish complicated maneuvers before landing.

- quarter pipes—these are basically one half of a mini ramp or vert ramp. You can ride up to it and do a trick before riding away. Quarter pipes are ideal for practicing new moves.

Top Two Ramp Movies
- *Testimony—this inspirational DVD took five years to make. It charts Mat Hoffman's amazing career, but also features ramp and street riding by a host of other big riders.*
- *Expendable Youth, Expendable 2, and Expendable 3—loaded with some of the greats of BMX, including Dave Mirra, Ryan Nyquist, DMC, TJ Lavin, Chad Kagy, Taj Mihelich, and a list of other top riders.*

FLATLAND SKILLS

You do not need ramps, race courses, dirt jumps, or street obstacles to have fun on a BMX bike. All you really need is some flat ground (ideally smooth concrete or pavement) and a bike. With practice, riders develop seemingly impossible skills of balance and technique.

This big-wheeled bike is designed for performing tricks.

Flatland Tricks

There are hundreds of tricks that can be linked together. Here are a few:

- endo—this is when the rider stops the bike, letting the rear wheel rise up in the air, and balances on only the front wheel.

- tailwhip—here the rider does an endo and follows it by swinging the bike around, usually through 360 degrees, keeping the front wheel still.

- 360 bar spin—in this, the rider stands on the rear foot pegs and holds the right handlebar grip with his or her left hand. Putting weight on the pegs to lift the front wheel off the ground, the rider then spins the handlebars through 360 degrees.

Great Flatland Movies
Diversion, Volumes 1–6—*this video magazine showcases cutting-edge flatland riding from around the world. You can also check out some of the material at the Diversion website: www.diversionvm.com*

Flatland riders need good balance to perform tricks such as this. This rider probably has fallen off hundreds of times before finally mastering it.

Viki Gomez from Madrid, Spain, has a good claim to being the world's best flatland rider. In 2002 and 2007, he won the Red Bull Circle of Balance contest, and in 2010 he won the BMX Flatland World Circuit series. Gomez is famous for coming up with new moves.

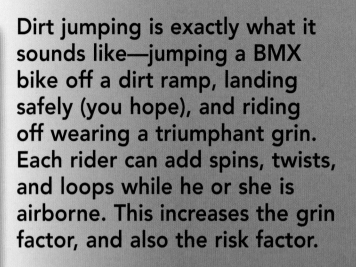

Dirt jumping is exactly what it sounds like—jumping a BMX bike off a dirt ramp, landing safely (you hope), and riding off wearing a triumphant grin. Each rider can add spins, twists, and loops while he or she is airborne. This increases the grin factor, and also the risk factor.

The advantage of jumping over soft dirt like this is that, if you fall off, it probably will not hurt too much.

Dirt Jump Bikes

Jump bikes have longer **top tubes** than a normal BMX bike. They do not usually have pegs—these can make for an uncomfortable landing if you lose your bike in mid-air, then fall on them. The bikes have a reinforced frame, and sometimes they also have bigger wheels.

Types of Dirt Jumps

There are lots of different types of dirt jumps. They are sometimes linked together to make up a series of jumps riders can tackle one after the other. The most common dirt jumps are:

- doubles—two mounds of dirt that are used as the takeoff and landing ramps.

- tabletops—the tops of the takeoff and landing ramps are linked by a plateau of flat dirt.

- ski jumps—just a takeoff ramp with no particular landing spot. Ski jumps are usually on a slope, which makes the landing easier and safer.

A rider takes to the air in a performance of the Giant Bicycle Stunt Team Show.

ON THE SCREEN

Nyquist is one of the all-time great BMX riders. For a while he competed at the top level in all three main BMX disciplines: vert, street, and dirt. He is probably best known for dirt riding, and has many King of Dirt and X Games titles to prove just how good he is.

RYAN NYQUIST

BMX racetracks feature a whole collection of dirt jumps like the ones listed on page 21. Turn up at a practice day with a suitable bike, pay your entry fee, and you get to ride around the course with other BMXers. This might be why BMX racing is becoming increasingly popular.

How Contests Work

BMX contests usually consist of a series of rounds called "motos." The riders get points according to where they finish—one point for first, two for second, and so on. The rider with the lowest overall score wins.

An alternative contest structure is for riders to fight their way through rounds to a final, with only the top-placed riders in each round going through. This happened in the 2008 Beijing Olympics, where BMX became an Olympic sport for the first time.

Riders wait for the start gate to drop (see page 24) before a big, international BMX race.

Bikes and Equipment

You can use an ordinary BMX bike for racing, though normally with the foot pegs taken off. Bikes with 24 inch (610 mm) wheels are also used for racing—in fact this is almost the only place you see them. Racers have to wear a helmet, and gloves, elbow pads and knee pads are a good idea.

Two competitors take a jump wheel-to-wheel. They must stay balanced while in the air so that they do not lose speed when they land.

Reade is a multiple world BMX champion. She learned to race by competing against male riders. Uniquely, in 2001 she was ranked number one in the British Men's 19-and-over division—despite being female and only 17 years old. She is one of the hot favorites for gold at the 2012 London Olympics.

For BMX racing you need a combination of speed, power, and bike-handling skills. Avid racers start building up their skills at a very young age. The youngest race category is six years and under for boys and seven and under for girls. Some riders have been racing for five seasons before they reach their tenth birthday!

Making a Fast Start

BMX races start at the top of a ramp. The riders line up behind a start gate, and when it drops, they zoom down the ramp toward the first corner. Reaching it ahead of everyone else is called "making the holeshot." If you manage this, it means you get a clear run at the jumps, **berms**, and other course obstacles. You also do not have to worry about other people crashing into you, which makes it far easier to ride fast.

Overtaking

Riders who do not make the holeshot have to do some overtaking if they want to win the moto. The main ways to get past opponents include:

- making long jumps—jumping several obstacles at once is a lot quicker than jumping them one at a time.

- cornering quickly—by braking at the last possible minute and accelerating away from the corner superfast.

- picking a faster line than others through corners and along flatter sections of the course.

The riders out front have two big advantages in a race—they are leading, and other riders cannot crash into them.

Showdown in Beijing
At the 2008 Beijing Olympics the hot favorites for BMX gold were Shanaze Reade and Anne-Caroline Chausson. Chausson, a former world champion at downhill mountain bike racing, had come out of retirement for the Olympics. In the final, Chausson was just ahead of Reade at the last corner, before Reade clipped her back wheel and fell. Chausson won, becoming the first ever Olympic BMX gold medalist.

A key skill in BMX racing is to look ahead and not at the ground under your wheel or the riders around you.

BMX is really good for you. Riding keeps you in shape and improves your **coordination** and reactions. But BMX is a dangerous sport. It pays to make your riding as safe as possible.

This rider's gloves save him from painful scrapes as he lands on his hands. He will try to roll away from the fall to avoid serious injury.

Learn to Fall!

Experienced riders always try to roll through a fall, rather than just slamming into the ground. The rolling motion uses up some of the fall's energy. If they are able to relax their muscles as they fall, they are less likely to be injured.

Be Aware of Other Riders and Skaters

In a skatepark, there will probably be lots of other people riding or skating nearby. Riders have to wait their turn to go on ramps and other obstacles, and must never cut in front of others. It is painful and embarrassing to have to admit that you got injured crashing into someone else!

About now, this rider has started to wish he packed a parachute or wore some extra padding.

Make Steady Progress

The only way to get better at BMX is to try new tricks. But trying tricks that are much harder than anything you have done before is a shortcut to a big crash. The safest way to improve is to pick tricks slightly harder than, but similar to, ones you can already do.

Bike Safety
Checking your bike before riding is the most important safety precaution you can take. After all, if a wheel or foot peg comes off in the middle of a trick, it could be disastrous. Key things experienced riders check include:
- *wheels—are they on tight?*
- *chain—is it loose and in need of retensioning?*
- *frame—are the handlebars, foot pegs, and seat all secure?*
- *brakes—if the bike has brakes, are they working properly?*

A multi-function tool, such as this, is very useful for any BMX rider.

There are great places to ride BMX all over the world. Practically every town or city has a few places that are fun to ride. But where would you go if you could pack your bike and travel anywhere in the world? Here are a few places to check out:

Decoy, Devon, UK

In a small town in Devon, this surprising spot has separate areas for BMX racing, a skatepark, and dirt jumping.

Jugendpark, Cologne, Germany

One of Europe's top BMX venues, Jugendpark often hosts BMX World Championship contests. The series of dirt jumps under a huge bridge is particularly spectacular.

Copenhagen BMX track, Denmark

Copenhagen is Bike City—and that is official! The city has been given that name by the UCI, the organizers of cycling contests around the world. The BMX track has one of the highest start ramps anywhere, at 26 feet (8 m).

The Southbank Centre, London, is used as an unofficial skate park by skateboarders and BMX riders.

The Millennium Park in Alberta is open 24 hours a day and is free to get in.

Millennium Park, Alberta, Canada

The Millennium Park is said to be the world's largest outdoor public skate and BMX park. BMXers will find a massive variety of obstacles to practice on here.

Barcelona, Spain

The whole city is littered with good places to ride. One of the best is the Premia de Dalt track, which has a park, a flatland area, and dirt jumps. You will meet local riders who will probably be happy to tell you about other spots.

Woodward West (California) and Woodward East (Pennsylvania)

Woodward West and East first became famous as training camps for skaters, but they are now popular with BMXers, too. There are racetracks, parks, and street facilities at both camps.

London, UK

There are great BMX spots all over London, but one of the best known is the Southbank Centre, close to Waterloo Bridge. There you will find some of the best urban riders.

900 bar spin

trick in which the rider spins the handlebars (and front wheel) around two and a half times.

air

slang for height. BMX riders are said to "get air."

berm

a turn that is banked up, or raised, on one side.

circuit

another word for a BMX track.

coordination

the ability to do more than one action at the same time.

endo

trick in which the rider balances on the front wheel with the back wheel in the air.

fixed

single-geared bike where if the back wheel turns, the pedals are forced to turn too, whether the rider is pushing on them or not.

freewheel

bike gear that allows the rider to stop pedaling while the bike's back wheel is still going around.

full-face helmet

helmet that extends around the face and over the chin. There is a gap for the rider to see and breathe through.

grind

trick in which part of the bike (usually the pegs) slides along a surface such as a bar.

no-hands

trick done without holding onto the handlebars.

no-hands 900

ramp trick in which the rider spins the bike (and himself) through two and a half turns, while letting go of the handlebars.

quarter pipe

ramp that has only one slope. Essentially, a quarter pipe is one half of a vert ramp.

single speed

bike with only one gear.

top tube

upper tube on a bicycle frame.

vert ramp

ramp like half of a giant pipe, with vertical sides.

Organizations

Union Cycliste Internationale
The UCI is the world governing body for BMX racing. Get all the info at www.uci.ch.

Competitions

X Games
This is probably the biggest freestyle BMX contest in the world, organized by ESPN, with competitions in both summer and winter. The Summer X Games features BMX contests for big air, vert ramp, and park riding. Catch up with the latest contests, rider biographies and videos at www.espn.go.com/action/blog?sport=xgames.

Dew Tour
Big name riders compete in most events on this tour. Check out tour info at www.allisports.com/dew-tour.

Websites

www.angelfire.com/ak3/baja/tricks.html
Do you know your Firehydrant from your Squeakerson? This site has excellent, clear explanations of these and lots of other BMX trick names.

Diversion Magazine
www.diversionvm.com
Diversion is an online flatland BMX magazine, offering excellent free advice and video demonstrations of how to do flatland tricks.

INDEX